WEEKLY WR READER
EARLY LEARNING LIBRARY

Let's Read About Dinosaurs

Giganotosaurus

by Joanne Mattern
Illustrations by Jeffrey Magniat

Reading consultant: Susan Nations, M.Ed., author/literacy coach/ consultant in literacy development

Science consultant: Philip J. Currie, Ph.D., Professor and Canada Research Chair of Dinosaur Palaeobiology at the University of Alberta, Canada

Please visit our web site at: **www.garethstevens.com**
For a free color catalog describing Weekly Reader® Early Learning Library's
list of high-quality books, call 1-800-542-2595 (USA) or 1-800-387-3178 (Canada).
Gareth Stevens Publishing's fax: (877) 542-2596

Library of Congress Cataloging-in-Publication Data

Mattern, Joanne, 1963-
    Giganotosaurus / by Joanne Mattern.
      p. cm. — (Let's read about dinosaurs)
    Includes bibliographical references and index.
    ISBN-10: 0-8368-7696-2   ISBN-13: 978-0-8368-7696-3 (lib. bdg.)
    ISBN-10: 0-8368-7703-9   ISBN-13: 978-0-8368-7703-8 (softcover)
    1. Giganotosaurus—Juvenile literature. I. Title.
    QE862.S3.M33225   2007
    567.912-dc22   2006029987

This edition first published in 2007 by
Weekly Reader® Early Learning Library
An Imprint of Gareth Stevens Publishing
1 Reader's Digest Rd.
Pleasantville, NY 10570-7000 USA

Managing editor: Valerie J. Weber
Art direction, cover and layout design: Tammy West

Printed in the United States of America

2 3 4 5 6 7 8 9 10 10 09 08 07

Note to Educators and Parents

Reading is such an exciting adventure for young children! They are beginning to integrate their oral language skills with written language. To encourage children along the path to early literacy, books must be colorful, engaging, and interesting; they should invite the young reader to explore both the print and the pictures.

Let's Read about Dinosaurs is a new series designed to help children read about some of their favorite — and most fearsome — animals. In each book, young readers will learn how each dinosaur survived so long ago.

Each book is specially designed to support the young reader in the reading process. The familiar topics are appealing to young children and invite them to read — and re-read — again and again. The full-color photographs and enhanced text further support the student during the reading process.

In addition to serving as wonderful picture books in schools, libraries, homes, and other places where children learn to love reading, these books are specifically intended to be read within an instructional guided reading group. This small group setting allows beginning readers to work with a fluent adult model as they make meaning from the text. After children develop fluency with the text and content, the book can be read independently. Children and adults alike will find these books supportive, engaging, and fun!

— Susan Nations, M.Ed., author, literacy coach, and consultant in literacy development

Look at this big dinosaur! Its name is Giganotosaurus.

Giganotosaurus was about as long as three minivans. Giganotosaurus weighed as much as four cars. It was as tall as two men.

Giganotosaurus was a fierce hunter! Its good sense of smell helped it find other dinosaurs to eat.

Giganotosaurus could run fast. Its speed also helped it catch other dinosaurs to eat.

Long, sharp teeth lined
its big jaws. They helped
Giganotosaurus bite and
eat other animals.

13

Giganotosaurus had long back legs. Its arms were short! Look at the sharp **claws** on its fingers and toes.

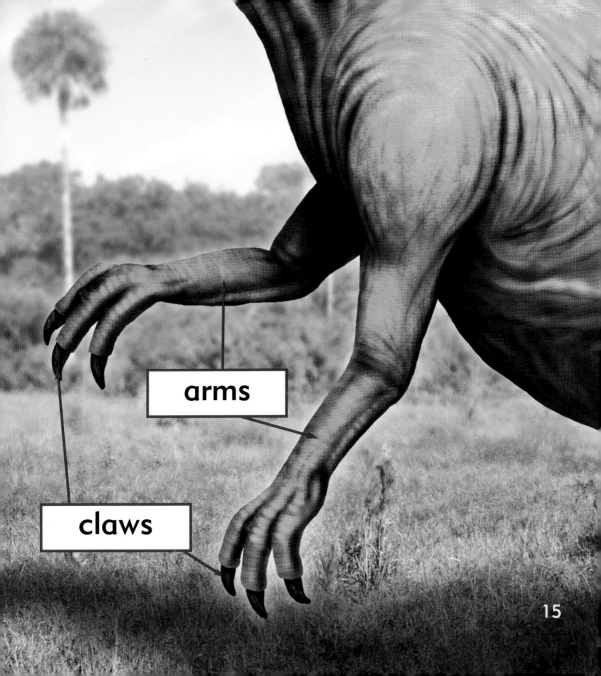

arms

claws

15

Scientists think Giganotosaurus may have hunted in packs. Lots of Giganotosaurus could kill a bigger dinosaur.

Scientists did not know about Giganotosaurus until 1994. Then scientists found this dinosaur's bones.

Today scientists are looking for more Giganotosaurus fossils. They hope studying this dinosaur will tell us more about the past.

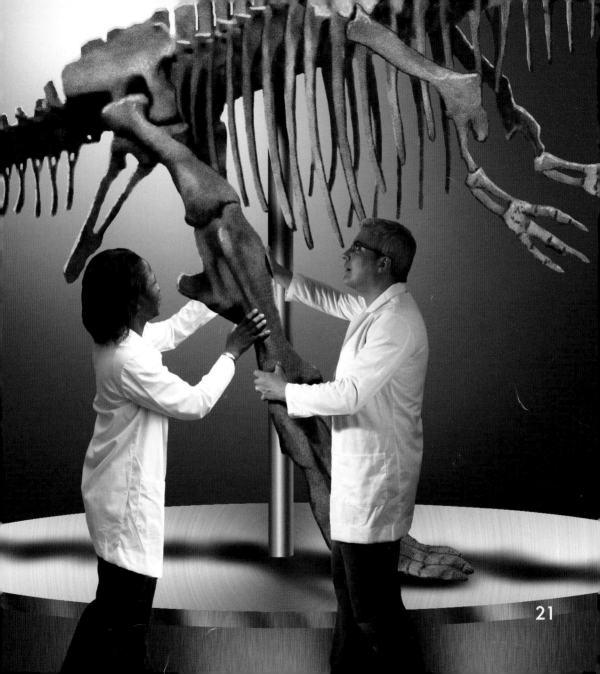

Glossary

fierce — strong and dangerous

fossils — bones or remains of animals and plants that died a long time ago

Giganotosaurus — a huge, meat-eating dinosaur. You say its name like this: jig-a-NOTE-o-SAW-rus.

scientists — people who study nature

For More Information

Books

Dinosaurs Big and Small. Let's-Read-and-Find-Out Science (series). Kathleen Weidner Zoehfeld (HarperTrophy)

Dinosaurs! The Biggest Baddest Strangest Fastest. Howard Zimmerman (Atheneum)

Giganotosaurus and Other Big Dinosaurs. Dougal Dixon (Picture Window Books)

New Dinos: The Latest Finds! The Coolest Dinosaur Discoveries! Shelley Tanaka (Atheneum)

Web Site

Zoom Dinosaurs: Giganotosaurus
www.EnchantedLearning.com/subjects/dinosaurs/dinos/Giganotosaurus.html
Here are lots of facts and drawings about this giant dinosaur.

23

Index

About the Author

Joanne Mattern has written more than 150 books for children. She has written about weird animals, sports, world cities, dinosaurs, and many other subjects. Joanne also works in her local library. She lives in New York State with her husband, three daughters, and assorted pets. She enjoys animals, music, going to baseball games, reading, and visiting schools to talk about her books.